My Husband Would

My Husband Would

POEMS

Benjamin S. Grossberg

UNIVERSITY OF TAMPA PRESS

Manufactured in the United States of America
Printed on acid-free paper ∞
First Edition

Cover painting: "Two Men on a Bench" by Arnold Lakhovsky (1880-1937)
Image courtesy of Heritage Auctions, HA.com
Cover design by Joshua Steward

The University of Tampa Press
401 West Kennedy Boulevard
Tampa, FL 33606

ISBN 978-159732-181-5(hbk.)
ISBN 978-159732-182-2 (pbk.)
ISBN 978-159732-183-9 (ebk.)

Browse & order online at
http://utpress.ut.edu

Library of Congress Cataloging-in-Publication Data

Contents

❧

In Medias Res   1

❧

Heaven   7

The Magic of Macy's   10

The Club, Houston   15

Days of 1993, '94, and '95   19

An Apology   20

The Dogs of Sochi   23

Grandmother at the Stove   24

Facing It   25

Rosacea   29

My Mother's Novel   32

The Finish Carpenter   39

I Go There   41

Math's Punishment   44

Whose Eyes Dart Contagious Fire   48

Afterward   51

Catherine the Great   54

Catawba   56

Pinnacle   58

Cody   63

Thanksgiving at Mom's, That   64

Perhaps Because I Am Youngest   66
Purgatory   69
The Next World   72
My Daughter Would   73
In My Forty-Seventh Year   76
The Hummingbird   79
Unemployments   80
To the Gentleman Who Asked for $500
    to Cap My Chimney   82
Praxis   86
A Thought   87

꙳

I Marry   93

꙳

Acknowledgments   97
About the Author   99
About the Book   100

For Sonia,
your book.

My Husband Would

In Medias Res

My face is the aftermath of my face. It is a face
after the big rumble. The buildings of my face
are upward exhalations of dust. There will be
aftershocks in the aftermath of my face.

I have the aftermath of brothers. Three of them.
The aftermath of brothers is a tunnel
dug through the floor of a prison and under
the guard tower and fence with a spoon.

The spoonfuls of dirt are childhood days,
and you eat them. The tunnel is quiet.
The aftermath of brothers involves dinner
every few years, and, sometimes, email.

I also have the aftermath of lovers. The aftermath
of lovers is like the surface of the moon: a gray
pulverized uniformity made of singular impacts.
My face and I are the aftermath of lovers.

The aftermath of sex is love, but usually briefly.
The aftermath of love is interminable.
My life is the aftermath of my childhood,
and I am the aftermath of my mother's life,

which means my mother's life was my childhood,
and that's eerily true. Teaching is the aftermath
of learning. Writing is the aftermath of reading.
The aftermath of friendship may well be

better friendship, but I haven't gotten there.
Which means the aftermath of friendship lives
in Minneapolis, and though I have long
forgiven him, I can distinguish no road back.

So the aftermath of friendship is that certain
kinds of conversations become theoretical.
The aftermath of a dog is a tin box. The aftermath
of a dog may also be a cat. The aftermath of a dog is

another dog is another dog is another dog,
and in that way dog attains something
like immortality. Except when it doesn't, then
the aftermath of dog is a cat. Or getting home late

and heading right up to bed. The aftermath
of chocolate is the aftermath of my face.
The aftermath of my face is a permbulating diet.
The aftermath of having had parents

is a constricting understanding
of them. Surely the aftermath of something
is a prologue. But maybe, because it's a prologue,
you can't know until the aftermath. The aftermath

of a car is an insurance check. The aftermath
of a car is—what's that word?—*historicity*.
The aftermath of a car is another car. Sometimes
a better one. But the aftermath of a man may be

no more men.

Heaven

The Houston nightclub, long shut down, where
I once spent Friday nights

Someone shoots up Heaven,
both bars and the small
dance floor in the back.
But the patrons, all just
my memories now,
ethereal, wisps of smoke
and soul, don't notice
or care. The bullets
spray through them
where they cluster at
the second bar, blurring
their bodies as they flirt
and throw back cocktails
that turn to vapor
in their mouths.
Heaven's dance floor
is a sway of boys. It's still
early nineties here,
so pastel disco lights flash
to "Strike it Up" and "100%
Pure Love." Patrons dance

as only memories can,
pressing so close they pass
through each other
at the lips. When bullets glide
through them, their bodies
mingle at the entrance wounds.
Fridays, cover charge
is a canned good, a donation
for the local soup kitchen,
and booze, a pour of smoke
in a plastic cup, costs only
fifty cents till eleven.
On a night like this, sultry, with
boys lined up to enter, a can
of Kroger peas or hominy
in hand, the click
click click of an empty
magazine, his last, is lost
to disco. He throws down
the gun, its cold solidity,
and charges the crowd.
But the boys turn to mist
still laughing at their own jokes
and settle once he's passed.
Spent, he collapses unnoticed

against and through
one of Heaven's walls
and tumbles right out of it.
At the bar, one of the boys
drifts toward another
a few stools down, the swirl
of him blown back
by the movement.
All night, he's been watching
a guy—Michael—who he
will continue to love
long after they've parted ways.
He's just found the courage
to go up and say hello.

The Magic of Macy's

A face like light, so much so that now
I wonder if he was albino or had vitiligo,
except that he had freckles and his hair
I remember was pale red and his eyes
pale blue: and tall, a good foot taller
than I was—am—with an unnoticing grace.

I am nineteen, standing behind the Coach
counter at Macy's Herald Square.
This feels like my first real job: I take
a bus to the city; I wear a suit.
I ask strangers if I can help them
even though I actually can't help them

since I know so little about leather goods.
But I want to help. I am clean-shaven,
virginal, terrified, thrilled, alternatively
self-conscious and dazzled into out-of-
body experience. I float above Coach
to see before me the grandeur

of Herald Square, and myself, tie knotted
once by my father, then carefully removed

each night by me to preserve the knot.
Around me is Men's, around me
is Macy's, around me is Thirty-Fourth,
and Manhattan, and I lean forward

over the glass, breath held, waiting
because I have an inchoate sense that
this is life, and that New Jersey, where
I'm from, is not, is in fact the holding pen
before life, where life—a bull with its balls
tied too tight—somehow doesn't buck.

Yet nothing happened that summer.
I was initiated into nothing.
I knew enough to understand there were
other experiences, places nearby
I could legally walk into where all
manner of consumption was possible:

there were hours after hours, spaces
to spend the night that didn't involve
taking the bus back to New Jersey.
Let's be clear: we're talking
men, multiple men, and drugs,
nighttime as a method of operation

with a range of textures that still,
twenty years later, I have admired only
behind glass: the price tag, the softness
of the leather, the "grain" we called it
as if it were a kind of wood, the once-
living skin that, cared for, lasts decades.

Truth is, I waited behind that counter
for life to walk up and extend its long finger—
the three-jointed bones of a skeletal hand
or something simian, the dark, knuckly
digit of an ape—tap down hard
on the glass, then turn swiftly, drawing me

Pied Piper-like after. My supervisor,
a jowly fifty-year-old with a lisp and a gap
in his front teeth, did ask me to dinner,
and I refused with a silent, emphatic
shake of the head. But aside from that,
summer wore on, showing me nothing.

Except once. The day he walked in,
my nearly elfin redhead. But he is not elfin.
Though impossibly tall and graceful,
his chest is wide, defined. He doesn't

look at me, just down at the glass, his long
red eyelashes combing over his eyes—

just barely blue, like watercolor diluted
to the point where it runs down the page.
A man is with him, also impossibly tall,
also with a wide chest, small waist, though
darker, and as the redhead looks through
the glass I stand before, the second man

leans softly against him and smiles.
Do I desire them? At first glance, you might
assume we are different species: fleshy,
awkward thing that I am, my bloated
tie knot and Bar Mitzvah suit, awkward
trundling thing smearing the counter glass

with his palms; and them like palm trees—
cool, tropical, a sure sign you are somewhere
you can't long afford to stay. I do speak
to them. I ask if they want to see something;
I ask, are they shopping for an occasion.
Then I try to think of something else, but

the red-haired one shakes his head slightly
and turns away without making

eye contact. His companion follows,
and they stroll off together, in love,
as I imagine, together from some country
where men are all built on that scale, where

skin is that clear and lashes always auburn,
a mountaintop place where humans grow
longer and more graceful in the thinner air.
It seems they have come down to meet me
over the glass barrier between us,
to show me something of life since I have

in fact bused all the way up from Marlboro
and walked over eight blocks among a crowd
from Port Authority. *You can get this
close*, they seem to say—the redhead's
eyelashes sweeping down as he looks
past me to the glass. *You can get just this close.*

The Club, Houston

No way to know now if I read about it
or lived it. Or saw a film in which

a young man, twenty-three, naked, glides
in a clear pool, his body nearly fixed in aspic.

On the patio above him, older men drink,
languid in the subtropical night—

Houston, 1993. Two, three, four AM. The club
is all but abandoned, but the showers

are going hot, and a single male voice, raspy
as the scratch of a child's violin, calls

over and over from the dark block
of steam. *Yes, thank you, oh god thank you.*

The halls are lined with doors. Some
are cracked open, their light spilling into,

brightening the hall. In one, a man, eyes shut,
lies on his back. His face and skin

redden with steam. His chest, shaved as close
as a jawline, beads with it. Occasionally,

a man wrapped in a white towel passes
through the hall or places an open palm

on one of the doors, pushes it, disappears
inside. And outside: the patio.

No music, no chatter. Just the men splayed
in the dark, their bodies rippling over onto

themselves. And in the water, the young man.
He circles, parts it so cleanly it forms

a sheen of glass around him. It must be true—
I hadn't realized until now—that

the young man isn't real. I don't mean
he isn't real to the men on the patio,

though that must be true, too. To them,
a set piece, a television at an airport

or suspended over a bar. Nor do I mean he is
unreal to himself—though perhaps that's

also true, that he knows himself a bathtub toy,
a wind-up shark that will run down grinding

out its own movement. No, I mean he is unreal
in a larger sense, uninhabited, a cypher,

that no one recalls being inside him now,
no one now can say whether there was

a young man in the pool or if they just
imagined him there. Or if he imagined

himself there, from a small bed in
a Houston side street, first-floor apartment

beneath a tower of yellow brick. No one
saw him slide from his clothes into the water

or glimpsed the underside of his body,
face, chest, genitals. No one can confirm

that he had a face, wasn't as featureless
as a manikin or a cool dish of wax.

All the other men are gone now. Scattered,
dead. The hallway doors shut, the facility

long since bleached clean and closed.
And even I who write this can't attest

to a single detail, though I do still hear, as if
from a nearby room, a raspy voice calling

from the steam, the sound divorced from
any other sound, from any shuffling of bodies,

and nearly desperate in its gratitude—
Thank you, oh god thank you, yes.

Days of 1993, '94, and '95

The Montrose Clinic, Houston

Timing; the lag. You couldn't know. Well, you *could.*
The slip in your wallet. The gravel lot—
a trailer, weeds, no sign. Your blood
drawn up, stoppered, a cotton-ball blot
band-aided to forearm. You could. You could
match numbers on test tube and slip, return
in two weeks. Wait three months. The lag. More blood,
new slip. You careful? Are you? Good. Or learn
—what? Discipline: to take yourself in hand.
Not so hard, right? But look: you're back in that chair,
forearm slung forward, dammed with a purple band,
new slip crammed in your pocket, thinking where,
how it might have gotten in—that tainted cell—
and wondering who you could and couldn't tell.

An Apology

For Joe

I know you've heard this before.
In the waiting room, I'd imagine
red Xs over some of us,
slashes across our torsos
visible only to a large, ripe

eye peering through the roof.
First there was waiting, then
there was more waiting, and that was
before we had to wait two weeks.
It wasn't the thought of getting

infected—not just that. But how
the self would become a plate
held at a careless angle,
its contents slowly sliding off.
With a dog circling, circling.

And then once, I drove home
from a man's house in tears. But
nothing bad had happened to me.

He'd told me on his couch,
our feet entangled. A gentleman,

he'd said it before the first
article of clothing hit the floor.
Amazing that it went further,
me more wick than fuse
even then, that the salt

crusted from a day walking
the Galveston sea wall—
how his skin held onto it—
is something I can still
taste. It made me pull sharply

back—*what is that?*—before
coming close. And last week,
you told me over the phone.
In response, I teased out your story,
avoiding the implicit question

about us. Yes, I knew how
you took it, my demeanor, such
news-anchorly interest.
It turns out something bad
did happen to me, didn't it?

And it was only later that I realized
your words, even your tone,
sounded practiced. Or no, not
practiced. Like something you'd
actually said many times before.

The Dogs of Sochi

In preparation for the 2014 Winter Games

Shot with poisoned darts, tossed in trucks.
Can you imagine that? The questing snout
snapping back toward the stung flank, the flux
of rising pavement, two-legged blur, a shout
before you're hefted by front legs, thrown
on a pile of your kind—the cold, sour tang
of death encircling, theirs and your own—
and then, perhaps, nothing. But one sprang
free—the news said one—small, red, prick-eared—
the dart dropped off, she shook, bolted the mound
of bodies, leapt out, hit the street, heard
them scrambling after and shot from the sound.
Just one. You taste the air rushing on her tongue,
the push of blood and breath, a running song.

Grandmother at the Stove

She strikes a Diamond on the box. It flares—
and when it nears the jet, a burst of blue
engulfs her hand. Seems to. But unaware,
she lets her hand linger, the match aglow
within the jet, bright as a tiny star.

Now she withdraws the hand, shaking, slow,
unfazed, and holds the match aloft in air—

then leans in close, face, lips pursed to blow.
The nub flickering, her forefinger and thumb
look like a wick, as if the fire had sprung
from her breath and she could carry it, numb
and wielding. At her knee, I watch, too young

to know she's come through three wars unburned.
What it means to handle fire, how she learned.

Facing It

Had I known I'd become
a Hasidic Jew, I might just
have gone religious
from the word go: beliefs
change, but a face is destiny.
Should I have realized that?
Say my nose is getting bigger,
my back bent: hook with a hook,
a caped Shylock insisting
on his profits and the full
force of law. My eyes, too,
moving closer together,
facial features
drifting like continents
on the globe of my head.
With a few more decades,
everything will be massed
in the center of my face,
a Gondwanaland of clumped
sockets with the Everest
of my nose breaking
the cloud line. As a child,

only once did I meet
my father's father. He:
white beard to the waist,
payot like the rope
of an ocean-going vessel,
black hat, black coat, he
drew me onto his lap
and blessed me through lips
hidden behind white-
straw thatch, his mouth
only a black opening
in the hoar frost.
He said blessings in
another language,
then, closing his fist
over mine, caused two
silver coins to fill my palm
before raising his hands
so I could be lifted off.
No doubt the old man
saw in me a Jew seed,
hard, green, unripe
fruit of a Jew to be left
on the branch
for the whole of the season

until it ripened into
a sweet Jew. And the silver
and those words in another
tongue? Who knows
what he was incanting—
he might have been telling me
to go live with the *shiksas*
awhile, to sin in all the ways
a body can. He might
have been prophesying
a time in my 40s when I'd
look in a mirror and see
a room full of chanting,
women separated out,
and sex so modest
a sheet intervenes.
Isn't it a kind of cruelty
to a child? Letting
the little bastard think
he's won, with a small
smirk of superiority
visible if one could only
discover your lips?
I still have the coins:
half-dollar and quarter

like something dredged up
from a chest in a cratered
ocean freighter. No skeleton
guarding it. Just an old
man with an old black hat,
old black coat, and an eye
that pegged my face decades
before it was mine.

Rosacea

All those years I condescended to my mother's face,
as if it were lesser than mine, as if it had marred itself:
her face's failures all failures of will—as if her face
had neglected to pay child support and instead
went to the track. As if her face had been fired
as a dishwasher from every restaurant in town, and now
I stood over it, hands on my hips or shaking a finger.
My face, you understand, was perfect. My face
was a glass slipper held out by a prince in a dinner
jacket sparkling with epaulets. My face was so fine
that once—this was 1994, Houston—I walked into
a bookstore and the cashier left his register, walked
right up to me, ran his thumb down my cheek—
unannounced, as if I were a public-park statue—
and asked, *What kind of foundation do you wear?*
See? My face had a right to be lordly: think fine
plaster spackled to make the walls of a dome on which
a master will paint the pink flush of biblical figures—
all that unfallen flesh, the rolls, handfuls unmarred
by even a simple pimple or birthmark, the brown
splatters that are so easily figured as sin.

My father was an accomplice in this haughtiness.
His cruelty bloomed on the topic of my mother's face.
He, too, saw the face as blameworthy and pointed out
the textures and discolorations as byproducts
of booze. He told her face it looked like a drunk's,
the nose and cheeks scarred up. And it *did* look
like a drunk's, though also like the surface of a red
moon roughened by centuries of comet impact,
the dry riverbeds and craters. He and I tag-teamed
the face, though my part was silent; my fine skin
and I, we held aloof, attacking merely with altitude.

My mother, of course, came to the aid of her face.
She would pick it up from wherever it was lying—
on a pillow, say, like a ceramic mask left there
for safe keeping—and curl it under an arm.
Sometimes she was drunk, it's true, and that didn't
help her face's case any. Tumbler of vodka in hand
and occasionally swung wildly, her face pressed
close to her chest like a sacred book, she slurred out
a whirlwind at my father and me, and we deserved it.
When things finally quieted down, she would take
her face upstairs to bed, but there were a few instances
when she did not, and I, later, would observe it
passed out on the couch, the curly blond hair
falling around it, and think that, for all its explosions,

splotches, and scars, that it still—in sleep—
had the sweet fleshiness of a child's, a little girl's face,
and it was easy to imagine it sleeping beside a doll.

Well, it's decades later now, and we go back to visit—
my face and I—both changed, reddened and pebbled
by time. When I'm there, I put my face right
beside my mother's, stack them like bowls. There isn't
daylight between them. I never drink, never have;
it seems drink was always a red herring. I don't
defend my face or even apologize to her face
for all my years of perfect skin and a smug bearing.
I let my face—from wet to dry, the varying hues
of Georgia clay—speak for itself. For her part,
my mother never brings up the past, either.
We sit at the kitchen table and let our faces enjoy
a little fellowship. No need to explain or apologize.
You know how it can be when people share a history.

My Mother's Novel

The protagonist's shift is soaked in kerosene—to remove a stain—
and this results, next day at school, in a peeling scald that she will
remember for decades. Arriving home, she lifts the shift from her
back, and flakes fall around her that she slowly realizes are skin. Then
her own mother's arms folded, lips tight, and the single nod that
stands in for pages of rationalization. This story may be apocryphal,
but as my mother types it, in the small, pink sewing room off the
kitchen, she lives it, as if she's drawn a picture of a swimming pool,
then reached a hand in, through the cool surface, up to her wrist.

❧

I am it. I am a placeholder
for it. I am a substitute
(poor?) for it. I am it
sublimated. I am its failure
phoning on Fridays, its voice
unintentionally
mocking. I am

an unprovable hypothesis and

at a certain temperature
melt into her words, bob
in the glass of them—
an ice cube. She sits at the table,
stirring a tumbler of vodka with
her pinkie. No, that's not her
anymore. Rather, tiny feet
up on the chair across from her,
Flaubert in one hand, half
a dollar-store cookie
in the other, she bites
carefully with one of her
good teeth. Then she turns
a page; I grow smaller.

❧

I am to buy her Tolstoy.
She insists: a scholarly edition.
She must have annotations!

❧

Mira mira mira. The protagonist, sixteen, walks down a side street.
She is still, as she was as a child in Eretz Yisrael, overweight. But—and
my mother lingers over the irony, she's very good at irony—she doesn't

yet know that weight has redistributed to hips, breasts. Breasts her
schoolbooks now flatten, tight in her arms. *Mira chica chica chica.*
To stop might be never to start again. And who on the street would
notice her disappearance? It's 1957, Denton, Texas, and the defining
element is dust. Cars or horses? Cars and dust. Each time a car passes,
a cloud of it kicks up and swallows the three men on the corner, their
crooked, darkened teeth, the brown leather of their arms. But their
voices pierce through. *Mira mira chica chica chica.*

&

Writing is a crack
that widens itself.

Let's unpack that, shall we?

My mother's awareness
has emerged, subterranean octopus,
through a cleft in the earth—
first two tentacles, wiry and flailing;
they dig and scrape the crack
wider, making space
for the squishy head.

Now it can come and go as it pleases,
at night, prowling the city

for children and old people,
squirreling them back
into the earth, to make of them
plot development.

I will not feel guilty.
I will not make useless comparisons.

But surely her books would have
sold better than mine. Which is to say,
at all.

☙

She does research. Could a single mother, a nurse, raise four children in Jersey in the mid-eighties? How much would an apartment in Marlboro cost? Does Marlboro have apartments?

No, it is not possible.
She must kill one of the children.

Is the protagonist's finger broken? He has yanked her wrist with his left hand, pulled off the ring with his right. Then the back of his arm slamming the bathroom door open and the tiny plunk of splashing water, like a single piano key.

Then a toilet flush.

On the couch, in half-light. The toilet has been removed, and, up to his forearm, he's reaching through the wax ring: a black hole in the house she hadn't known existed, interface with another realm. There is, it turns out, a clear horizon from beyond which things cannot be recalled. *If you need to use the bathroom, use the one upstairs!* she announces. Three children peek out like prey animals from behind trees. A few minutes later, they eat hot dogs, squeezing the fluffy buns together as they bring them up to their mouths. Their plates piled high with chips. Eyes on the screen.

The protagonist will make the harder choice. And, late at night, she will write.

℘

My mother puts my book on the table,
facedown, still open, making of it
a lean-to. She looks up at me, over
the top of her glasses, which balance
impossibly far down on the tip
of her nose. She pauses, holding
the moment's attention.

Soon: a zinger.

∞

You haven't read Tolstoy? she stammers, shocked. *Not
even Steinbeck?*

My answer is the verbal
equivalent of shuffling feet.

∞

The protagonist, older, a successful novelist, speaks at the commence-
ment ceremony of a small private liberal arts college—one of those
peppy anachronisms. She discusses two roads that were, she insists,
her fist hard against the podium, the same road: to minister to the
very old or very young.

The Chinese menu of her life—
Mother/Spinster. Teacher/Nurse.

A folding chair in the first row—purposefully left empty—represents
the possibility of me. Just in case the unbirthed spirit visits, like the
cup left out for Elijah.

She insists on this at all speaking events.

∞

Two roads that were the same road—
and she, by temperament, no better suited to either
than I would be.

So she writes; I write her writing
late at night now, a single light on
in the sewing room off the kitchen.
(She's onto something good.)

The Finish Carpenter

Half million, and what? Cardboard subfloors—
crap, but all right. Vinyl-sided chimney.
Looks like shit, but can't be seen indoors,
that's something. But, Jesus, what you *can* see:

door frames, wall openings, kitchen pass through—
no moldings. Nothing. It's like a face
without eyebrows. Or ears. And we're talking new
construction, nice street. There's window casing,

I guess we should be grateful. But they're my folks—
pop was an architect—and I say, look, Dad,
I'll bring my goddamned miter saw. He walks
away from me, shaking his head. Glad

to do it, I say. Take me a day. He shrugs;
I see his shoulders move, his hand sweep down
in front of his face like he's clearing bugs
or a smell. Why not, Dad? Just a little crown

in the den, some chair rail. He's seventy.
What happens—shit ceases to matter

at that age? Come on, I say. No filigree,
just finishing. You still have that step ladder,

right? He's on the couch now, remote in hand,
surfing. I don't get it. I don't. Fine
corners, cornice, some detail, a few planned
correspondences. Why not? Some lines

to guide the space, hold it together. It frames
the parts. Gives shape. An order. Some *wood*.
That's all I want for him. No games,
just shape, a little grace. He's my blood;

I want him to have it nice. *Mirrors and smoke*,
he says, not looking up. He's been saying it
to me twenty years, since I went broke
fixing my first place. Prewar, Sears kit

with nothing plumb, and me wild on the phone
raving about warped floor joists and plaster.
Smoke and mirrors, he said. And that's it. Done.
And me, ankles deep in my disaster.

I Go There

Probably it's safe to say that my mother

                                    never liked sex, though

on some level

                she must have wanted it. She'd wanted

babies—not necessarily

                        children. She told me that once with an

uncharacteristic dreaminess, even her pronunciation of the word

babies drawn out and hinting

                            at music. But sex was clearly

another thing, reserved, I gathered

                            peripherally, as children do gather,

after not too long

                    for vacations, where it could integrate seamlessly

with margaritas and those old plastic keychain photo boxes

where you put your eye to the lens and see

                                  your mother permed, your

father in a suit, leaning into each other in the dining room

of a cruise ship, beside

                    a table of strangers. There would be

dancing, too: father over a foot taller

                            swaying back and forth, mother

chugging her arms at her sides as if

imitating a choo choo, and then
back down for the chicken or the fish.
They haven't spoken, not
that I know of, in
fifty-five years of marriage, but it's entirely possible
that proximity itself communicates
something. He still sometimes
yells like a crack of thunder
loud enough to make a street seem to
tilt up toward you
at her, and at anyone who criticizes her. At 46,
I'm already too old to know
marriage like that. But sex
I do know, at
three- and six-month stretches, in a way they
never will. Yet surely they know enough of it—
if not in the act,
in the decades they had to
ponder its grievances. What other thing
could have beckoned them at
nineteen and twenty to marry?
I heard the story forty years later (again, peripherally), how
he'd run to Mexico after
and had to be dragged back by
both sets of parents: is it even
true? And from where did I hear

that he'd come back with—

                    but how to say this delicately—

an infestation? No,

               I'm sure she never liked it and sure he never

got what he liked: granted, my evidence largely humor's bitter

subtext

       flung, during commercials, across the couch, all but over

the heads of children, a snapped

                   rubber band. Last time

I attended a wedding with them, they were the final couple dancing

after the DJ

           finished winnowing by decades: a Mutt-and-Jeff

silhouette, her squat chugging, his awkward

                          swaying, charmed

to find themselves alone on the floor. They're not the people

they were in the bedroom, more likely backseat, that first time, and

maybe it's perversity in me that I prefer

                      to imagine that—a torrent

of appetite like wrestling salamanders, glossy

                   as egg yolks,

no idea that they would or could grow up to be

                   this: creaky

dancing become sex become dancing.

            I know nothing of love.

Math's Punishment

For Lucas

This is how I want to know your body.

In the *Mabinogion*, book of Welsh folklore,
the conjurer Math punishes two men, nephews
who had violated the woman whose job it was
to cradle his feet as he slept.
Math banishes the men to the woods for a year
and with a wave of his wand transports them
into new selves: into stag and doe—
their hard uprightness melting
to haunch and hoof.

One year later, the barking dogs
call Math back to the castle gate
to find stag, doe, and behind them now, shyly,
a fawn. Math kneels, beckons it forward,
and when he lays hands on it, it flashes
into a sturdy boy of twelve, blond, the book says,
and Math leads him in to be christened
Hyddwn, which means *Of Deer*.
And the nephews? It must have glimmered

in them then that they'd once been men,
a dilating human awareness—
the doe apprehending with a man's grip
the spaces in her body, what the other
had filled—quick-fire, unexpected wholeness—
and the life that had crowned there
like a secret passed between them
now telegraphed to the world.
And the stag, too: recalling a man's body

as his own had been, fallen to all fours
in front of him, the press of his hooves
on its back, how it drew him from himself
into its sheltering vortex, the haunches
he desired and continued now to desire, that
were and were not those of the man he knew.
But Math isn't done with them yet.
He returns to the gate, raises his wand,
and tumbles them back into the world

for another year, the stag rolling
into the body of a sow, what was pendant
drawing sharply back, and the doe
lifting itself up as a boar, all energy channeling
through and outside itself, and both animals

charging out to thicket and plain
to exchange knowledge, to pass it between
them in a language of grunt and muscle.
Another year goes by, and again

barking dogs call Math to the castle gate.
And there, waiting for him, are sow and boar,
and behind them this time a young pig—
which he kneels and beckons forward.
At his touch, it, too, flashes into an upright boy,
whom Math christens, Hychdwn, *Of Pig.*
Then he raises his wand and
—perhaps it comes slower now, a calculation
checked and re-checked, a sum which can't be

but is correct—the nephews find themselves
upright, human. Math declares their experience
a great disgrace, and they stand beside each other
naked and public as a vow, each scraped
bright, mud-covered; each with the crazed
beards and hair of hermits. In a daze, then,
they follow him back to the castle.
The gates shut. And the *Mabinogion* isn't
much concerned with them after that.

But is there, lover, in any other mythology
a pair like them?
Fallen and shamed, no doubt, but maybe
feeling something else, too—satisfaction, even
buried pride as they sit together at table
beside their sons, men in a family of men?
I think none at all—
though maybe Adam and Eve come closest,
Adam and Eve as they stumble

hand in hand out of Paradise, just
as the nephews must have
stepped forward, if a little too stunned
to hold hands, away from the animal world.

Whose Eyes Dart Contagious Fire

I'd like to convince you that it was
beautiful: he and I in a state park,
hidden by trees just off the cleared
space of a high-power line, tottering
against each other and still
mostly dressed. Can you believe
it was beautiful? Or innocent—
because it was that, too. Innocent:
the kind of warm November that
ignites spontaneous running. I ran,
and he tried to catch up, soon
leaping onto, tackling me, both of us
falling, out of breath and laughing.
If we were sixteen, if there was
a soundtrack, a pulling back and
panning of trees, if music "soared,"
wouldn't you describe the moment
as innocent? If one of us were
a high-school quarterback, the other,
shy, living out the template
of a crush; if she were shivering in
a long cotton shirt, sleeves pulled

over her hands, and he bundled her
in the leather of his coat, wouldn't it
be innocent, be beautiful? But two
middle-aged men by a power line,
on a second date, with our clothes
bunched around our midriffs, ankles—
what if I said it was twilight
and we tore apart from each other
to the shock of headlights, a siren,
that a cop came out of the vehicle,
angry, and a second angry cop—
one from each door—started
toward us: a *public* park. That's
what they were saying, hitting
the word like a nightstick
on an open palm, a *public* park.
Imagine us now, our hoods pulled
over our heads, cuffed, lowered
into the backseat. What if the shy
girl undoes her hair, takes off her
glasses, and even though she's cold
twirls away from the quarterback
like a ballerina, then he laughs, does
a mock twirl of his own, and holds
his hand out to her, as if they were

really going to start something
like ballet, only then they kiss
and the camera does its slow,
insinuating fade? In the backseat
of the cop car, he and I look down
to our knees, away from each other;
we are locked behind plexiglass,
hearing a voice swagger into the CB,
Coming in with a couple of fags, yeah,
at Johnson State, we caught them
pegging each other in the woods.
Except it didn't happen that way.
It was sundown, and we cleaned
each other with a crumple of leaves.
And walking back along the path,
we passed teenagers from the local
college—a couple, I think—probably
out there to get stoned or watch
the sunset. Likely both. And that,
too, is beautiful, is innocent, isn't it?
They looked up at us as we passed,
two middle-aged guys knocking
shoulders, holding hands, but they
didn't do a double take. The guy
nodded his head a little, the girl smiled.

Afterward

Two chairs back to back, a foot apart, and an afghan like a netting
over them. I ought to have told you.

One night, the radio—inches from my ear in a silent house—played
the Everly Brothers' "Dream."

You might, listening in bed beside me, have entered the story, our
child bodies lying side by side in the music.

I ought to have said: *One night, the Everly Brothers, a telescoping
darkness.*

As if the tent and I and the radio were falling down a hole, the hallway
bulb receding above us

but not the crooning, not the celestial harp-twang of guitars.

Lying in bed on an afghan. Telling you would have put you there,
and putting you there might have

kept you here. If I'd said, *Your body is comfortable to mine in a way
that makes me a dumb animal.*

If I'd described my body pressed on yours like an animal rounded in
its cavity of dirt.

And then the Everly Brothers, how we would have been kids under
the tent if I'd told you.

How, as I'd told it, you would have tumbled down the mine shaft of it,

your arms and legs out, but you slow in the descent and hear harp-
sounds and harmonies.

Then drift beside me feather-light, to where I lean on my elbows
listening, and music

becomes a ledge for us in a column of darkness. Those afghans; these.

But now, because in telling you the story, you have become part of it
and changed the past, now

the present changes. Now you are here talking about how, when we
were kids beneath the tent,

my body grew into yours in the way of things deep in the earth.

Not animals in a den. Deeper. The fine threads of roots, white and
eyeless.

Knotting. So close that I say, *When we were kids beneath the tent, it was then*

I came to love you. It was then as we listened to "Dream" and I told you

how for months as a kid I slept under a tent made of afghans

with you beside me, telling you about how I slept under a tent of afghans. It was then.

Catherine the Great

We're all undone by appetite; but which,
at least at first, is up to us. He pressed
himself against me in a parking lot.
We'd just finished our coffee and small talk.
A Sunday afternoon: cars pulling out
around us, and him salacious in my ear—
Catherine the Great. I didn't move. He ground
himself on me, cars swerving around the one
body we'd become. I couldn't move.
The potentate who died under a horse?
Prussian-born Russian Queen? A golden age
of Russian empire and enlightenment—?
He growled her name again, and I tumbled in
toward my center: my navel a sinkhole
into which all the neighborhoods of me fell.
The truss holding the ropes; the snap; the horse
whinny as its weight drops down; the snap
of Catherine's back; or neck; the world somehow
from Paris to British Hindustan at once
hearing it: *whinny, whinny, snap, snap*—
and a car horn: shoppers leaving Trader Joe's
can't be expected to wait out two men

for long, can they? Not quite in an embrace;
you wouldn't say *seemly*, wouldn't say
tasteful, certainly not with children close.

The moment captured for us is the break—
captured by rumor, by the pulley squeak
of invention—and maybe just before,
the illicit functioning, man and machine,
woman and horse, their factory passion.
Perhaps lost is the decade leading up,
when something, even in the world of myth
we'll never know exactly what, leaned in
close to Catherine, right off cobblestone
or pantry, whether breeze or beast or man
pressed itself up against her with a word
or name touching her bodice and lace,
the lips of it so near her skin that she did
some 18th-century version of what I did—
jumped into the car, hightailed it home
after saying, simply, *follow me,*
then waiting, hazards blinking, so he could.

He taught me Russian history—
                                                            in time,
you get crushed by the horse. Always crushed.
If you could, you'd get crushed by it twice.

Catawba

They do it overnight, the catawba tendrils,
reach and wrap the wire above them—
grow and curl, extend and expand. They reach
blindly because how else could they reach?
And find what they didn't know was there,
what's been arranged for them, the perfect
structure for their needs. Or as perfect
as this man could make it. What happens
in darkness, in a single evening—
let's not call it passion, not compare it
to human bodies, which also can reach, unseeing,
for each other; let's not think how conducive
the fixation. If I decide a tendril's not
landed right, I can undo it—carefully—maybe
half the time. The other times result
in damage. Let's not call it passion, not
compare it to how men can hold each other
in the dark, can coil each other's bodies
in a green fastness, the interlocking of a desire
more fierce than simple need. We know need;
we pass its debased currency daily. We know
what blandness its worship comes to. But do we

know this? Overnight, the instinctive triple
coil of a thin tendril, such fierce binding?
Let's not call it passion, not be implicated
in its dumb green living; not take it as just
another reminder from the natural world
of too much mind, how often it fails us.

Pinnacle

As if, breaking through the cloud line,
a vision of sunset—
the long red streams of light
defining, by approximation, infinity.
You exhale, though there's no way
to embed yourself more fully in the moment,
to set yourself in its mortar,
press down more firmly into your boots.

Your palm reaches out almost instinctively
for a hand. You don't look down;
your palm just feels outward

and finds his fingers.

I mean this as a figure, but I was on such a mountain once, my fingers
tendrilling out toward a man's. Though he and I never connected
very deeply, we found something together in the sunset: him relating
to its beauty, and me relating to its beauty, and though we could not
relate to each other, not after a year of trying, it was momentarily a
conduit, letting us experience a grandness together, if not in, or for,
each other.

On the cable car back, the weight
of our indifference didn't but might have
sunk the gondola low enough
to scrape the tops of evergreens.

⁊

Or, on the bed with the cat. She sits
on your chest, the soft ball of her head
nuzzling into your palm. She is
a gentle motor on your breathing,
vibrating I'm told at a frequency
that mends bone.
A breeze pushes in the sheers.

The phone rings.

And she yowls as if stuck by a fork,
back claws scraping your stomach
as she leaps off. *Crap* you think,
check the number—
snap the damn thing closed.

⁊

What the mind wants is a destination of moments, of pinnacle and pinnacle: an epic catalogue, a montage—that part of the movie where many weeks of training pass and we have an old but remarkably dense Sylvester Stallone jumping rope and punching a hung-up slab of cow.

Everything, even the shape
of his nose,
seems hewn from stone.

Montage: moment by moment, stitched.

☙

Or, in the dark car—a midnight drive from the farmlands north of Dayton into Cincinnati—another man taking my hand, advancing with such slow, cautious movement that I was unaware of his taking it, simply that at some point in the previous hour his hand had moved over mine.

I can't remember
in the decade following
him again saying
I love you.
He must have said it, but
I can't remember.

His words displacing highway noise.

(Like the cat slowly entering the room—
the noiseless step
that must have evolved to catch prey
but has found this other, more tender use.

Then the jumping off, the yowl.)

Suddenly his car pulls up the driveway,
his hand jerking away, the dome light
coming on, the sharp ratchet back
of an emergency break.

ॐ

The mind wants pinnacle drawn out, wants moments widening
on the surface of consciousness like a drop of oil. The mind wants
brothers, cat, this man and that one, this dog, and that other man as
we sat together at Panera: me underlining in a book, him sketching
something, then getting up to order a muffin. Later picking out the
chocolate chips one by one so I could eat them.

Every catalogue of loss
also a catalogue of having.

I should have, on the gondola down, reached across to take his hand
where he sat—told him that I loved him. Even if I didn't. Wanting
to love is a kind of love.

Not that love has much figured in the calculus
of what I have, thus far, been able to keep.

The mind wants not one—
but all, and simultaneously.

❧

Or, side by side on a mountain
with anyone. Any other hand, any other body
deriving its needed warmth from mine.

The mind wants and wants,

but it's a grim, nearly unbearable thought,
the fungibility
of what the mind wants.

Quiet. Or something beautiful.
Any hand, any mountain.
A you, a with.

Cody

You drove me through your childhood. Group homes
you ditched—one now a Noodle House—bus stations
that saw you to LA and back, tea rooms
that paid the fare. Strip-mall assignations
and rambling. Is that it, the core of you—
celibate, fifty, portly, six-figure job
but inside, stick-thin streetkid stoked on glue
scraping his hips against Sandia scrub?

A twenty-year friendship. But after the tour,
next day, you cut me off, full stop. The scalding
of your rage flung in my face. Why—what slight
or sulky fuss? My worst you'd seen before.
Did I miss it on that drive, some mauled thing—
if the streetkid knows, would he tell me for a light?

Thanksgiving at Mom's, That

Last time, that was nice, all of us there, and her sat sideways
on a chair, short of breath after bringing out the yams, a slab
in their thick Pyrex. And the last time I saw Michael naked
was nice because I noted the color of his skin—cream with one
tablespoon of coffee stirred in, that precise, one tablespoon—

and let my fingertips brush his leg as he began jumping up
in an attempt to wrench his jeans over his thighs. It was nice
watching him do his little jumps as he avoided my eyes.
Some people have strangely soft skin. What causes that?
Leaving the vet without the dog was nice. Driving home, taking

curves as sharply as I dared. Thinking I'd never be back
but of course I was a few years later with a cat. But
it was nice that last time, watching the final gust, all the air at
once issuing from the lungs like wind from the back of a very
deep cave, how it jittered the muzzle flaps on its way out.

There was a specialness since you knew it would never
happen again. Along with grieving. Grieving is grieving, but
this was a specialness. Like the flowering cherries—aren't they,
at the corner of Mountain and 44?—their blossoms
particularly nice against black bark, pink jade as if the car

had slipped into a Japanese painting and would soon ascend
the five brushstrokes that constitute, in far distance, a mountain.
Maybe thirty times left to see how nice they are. Thirty times
could make it a different experience than the very last time,
but how to know, now? And O Luke the last time we kissed

when I had come there to end it, the kiss just a cancellation
stamp on the mouth like at the post office, hard stamp, but
still time for a little give, a softness not love like how a player-
piano might not express feeling, but, in another room, who can tell?
Knowing it was the last time, that was extraordinarily nice. Then

we all sprang up, my brother lifting the Pyrex from her hands,
she twisting away from him. *I'm all right, I'm all right, I'm
all right.* So I should get out, right? Pull over and get out, reach
up to feel petals thick on the branch, not jade despite how
perfect they look, real petals. *Thirty, twenty-nine, twenty-eight. . . .*

Perhaps Because I Am Youngest

I am following you down a supermarket aisle.
I am following you down a sidewalk, the house models
with names that recall gentry: *Kilmer, Buckingham.*
Now we're riding a dusky Schwinn; I've been lifted

onto the back. Soon we'll tumble over like someone has
dropped the video camera, and the side of my cheek
will scrape open against the edge of the sidewalk.
But for now I am just behind you on the Schwinn—

a compelled following. It is always a compelled following.
Now I am following you down the hospital corridor.
You are on a gurney, a plastic mask being lowered
onto your face. I am following you, trying to understand

why the woman over you is counting. At the end
of the corridor is a large pit in the earth, and they will
slide you off the gurney into it. But first I follow you
to the kitchen. No, no, it's Penney's, and I follow you

to the changing room. I stop outside the door, waiting
till you come out in a denim wrap-around skirt which

I've tugged off the rack for you. You emerge and twirl,
making the skirt rise into a dinner bell. Now clothes

drape over your arm, and we approach the cash register.
I follow you in line, holding the skirt, and to the
Thanksgiving table holding a bundle of large, mismatched
spoons. You hold two bottles of soda. Now you hold a box

of matzoh and bottle of red wine. And a jar of pickles.
Or gardenia. You say it twice: *gardenia.* I follow you,
but now I have to sneak to the stairs and hide against
the railing to see you. Smoke in the air. A brightness

that is still the house. Sort of. A brown and orange
silk blouse that drapes over your breasts. I can see
the blouse, but I may not make any noise or follow you.
And once—but when, when?—I followed you

to the kitchen where you rolled sour-cream dough
for rugelach. As I watched, I grew to your ankles,
to your waist, till—unspooling like a tendrilled plant—
I curled over your head. Then I brought a tray

of rugelach, the crescents stuffed with chocolate, to
the couch where you lay under an afghan, and you lifted

your hand to stop me from bringing them closer. *No?*
I asked, pleading. And you shook your head no without

much opening your eyes.

Purgatory

What it's like—dinner table in the small
eat-in kitchen where my three brothers and I
will while away purgatory—
that will be up to us, whether light
through the slider doors is orange flame
that licks against the glass,
or blue sky that pushes on
the seams where walls meet, opening
the room's corners—impossible geometry—
into wider and wider angles.

Machines that can be fixed only by the workshop
that made them, toasters that must be shipped
back to the factory in Georgia—
is it even worth the postage?—that's us.
If we're smart, we'll resist talking.
That first sentence may
determine everything: the words
strung into a rope to ascend (knots only
for easy gripping) or a fuse, eternal, with
intermittent explosions to cover us
in psychological shrapnel, the viscous

fragments of our personalities flung hot
across each other's faces.
Think bowls of pasta, hurled.

I'm cagey. A learned trait. It won't be me
speaking first. I'll knit my fingers, keep
my head down. But soon I'll get drawn in, too.
Soon I'll also be pounding the table,
spittle launched to the opposite wall.
The really bad moment will come
when the first of us gets up to storm off—
tries to—and finds his posterior incorporated
into the seat, a seamless transition
from '70s-orange vinyl to skin.
It's then that the small details, the wallpaper—
burnt-orange tulips over a tan grid
that our mother puzzled over for months—
and the three different clocks,
will come to seem sinister. The tulips
like wands of flame. The clocks
like clocks.

But maybe we'll get past it. Maybe
some celestial mechanism will spur us forward.
Or maybe we'll be the mechanism: having
the same conversation over and over—

its rhythm, a Ravel's *Bolero*
of brotherly consternation, the bassoon
and trumpet of our voices culminating
in ringing walls. Maybe we'll play it out
in infinite variation until, somehow—
a thousand years, ten thousand—we stumble
on the right tone, hit the notes
that let us make a gentler harmony.

And then? The sliders open onto early May,
and the backyard gets transformed
into a massive lawn on a rolling hill—
a hunk of western Pennsylvania—
so we can look down into the endless
garden party, white tents, buffet tables, people
playing bocce in suits and gowns,
that is the whole of heaven. Our fellow dead:
friends, colleagues, people with whom
we can talk like normal, civilized adults.
Then our chairs detach from us, and we
walk out into the sun. Someone saunters over
to offer us punch, and we never
have to see each other again.

But we do anyway. If only once a year.
Because we want to.

The Next World

Three years gone, the dog will greet me there.
She'll waggle up to my arms at the pearly gate.
A Spitz with wet glass eyes and fine white hair,
she was nearly an angel in her earthly state—
with just as much free will as angels have,
her nature to please mine, to show how grace
can elevate obedience into love
and turn a wolf's into an angel's face.

But if things go south, at least there'll be my cat—
soot fur with eyes that flash like yellow tin.
She'll help the devils rend my flesh, a blur
of arch and hiss, of claw, ears back and flat.
She shows the gross indifference of sin
then implicates me with a little purr.

My Daughter Would

Eat McDonald's. Hate cats and refuse to pretend otherwise,
even with my cat whom she'd call "butt stain" and flick off
the couch with her thumb and forefinger. Be named
after Viola from *Twelfth Night* because I was delighted by

Bonham Carter in the Trevor Nunn film. Her friends
would call her Lola because she'd have somehow discovered
The Kinks. Would she know I hate that song? My first
boyfriend said *Don't bury me* when I observed we'd never

grow old together because of his HIV status. She'd have
dug his Wassily chairs—black leather strips over chrome,
which looked like torture devices or sex apparatus.
He insisted they were comfortable. She'd have

plopped herself down in one and stretched her arms
along the armrests, asking, *Where are you taking me for dinner?*
It would only have seemed like they were ganging up on me.
I'd have bought her books, a bicycle, skirts the color of

forest moss in rain, to match our eyes. A watch pendant—
1920s reproduction decorated with seed pearl.

She'd have wiped wrenches with the crenelated skirts,
rolled her eyes and never worn the watch, but kept it

with the diamond studs in the locked drawer of her desk
until she sold both to buy an old Prius, to visit Tijuana
after graduation. I'd know because I'd have kept a key
to the drawer, which I still wouldn't have told her about

even now, though she'd be a parent herself and doing
similar things. He once told me, my first boyfriend,
that the only loss he felt when he was diagnosed
was that he couldn't have kids. He and I spoke

that intimately in bed, which I'm not sure people
do anymore. *That's the thing you'll miss?* I thought,
incredulous. He curled his head on my shoulder,
and I said I hoped he'd miss nothing. *Viola, lower that shit*

music and shut your goddamn door. My own parents use
expletives compulsively—they're from New Jersey—
and did so throughout my childhood. One Seder, my brother
printed a picture of a woman fondling a gray stallion

and brought it to the table, where it rested on his Haggadah
until it caught my father's eye. My mother was serving

gefilte fish, a tan, pocked loaf in translucent mucous.
With current drugs, even if he and the mother were both

positive, he could—the baby would be protected. These days,
when I bring Viola home for Passover, it's disappointingly
sedate, but I'm unnerved anyway when she pokes
the gefilte fish with her finger, puts the finger to her mouth,

then eases a slice of the cold loaf onto her plate.
Since my mother and brother are eating it, too, I can say
nothing. Through the magic of Facebook, I know
he, at least, has found a husband. They recently redid

their kitchen in sleek checker-board marble. *Shut
your own goddamn door, Dad,* she screams from upstairs.
And it's Lola, okay? LOLA. Their stainless fridge
has no drawings taped to it, just like mine.

In My Forty-Seventh Year

Me walking downcast. Him dangling
ankle-level above a forest path with no
branches overhead. I glance to the canopy,
a good thirty feet up. Thirty feet. No
overhang closer. Let's pause for scale—
the caterpillar, half-inch long, and his silk
just a glint when wind sends it swinging
as if someone has, with an X-Acto knife,
cut a vector into the air. And above him,
a gulf of nothing. What human has scaled
such height, has been such a fantastically
attenuated pendulum? So I stop to watch
the shudder inside him. Is he consuming it
or balling the tether between rows of legs,
skeining it? Whatever he's doing, he's
clearly—and at a remarkable rate—
rising: the curl and lengthening of his body
steadying him higher and higher, so that
as I watch he floats from my ankles
to my knees to my waist, and in short order
we are eye to eye. It's then I think of fear.
At my ankles, it was nothing, the fall.

Even now, to me, not much. But soon
he will rise higher, to a height from which
I'd be terrified to suspend, to swing up
above the heads of couples strolling
hand in hand, with only that filament
and the wind-sway, its ocean-size capsize.
Impossible. So I look up again to gauge
the height, and see—because I'm awake
to them now, am looking now—a dozen
other caterpillars also rising, maybe end-
of-day rising back to the trees. For sleep?
But how to get the line up there unless
they've kept tethered all day as they
explored earth beneath them, like humans
walking the ocean floor, an umbilicus
waiting to reel them up. Yet this is height,
not depth, height: so like humans dangling
from skyscrapers—or no, not skyscrapers,
because no structures stand nearby, no
solidity at all, so like humans ascending
to clouds, a dozen humans inching up
on their own power, to the undersides
of clouds. And when I look back down
to find my caterpillar, I start because
he's gone, but soon see that he's not gone,
he's just above me now, four feet over

my head, tensing and ingesting his silk.
On this day when I've done nothing, when
a walk has seemed accomplishment enough
because I've lacked the will to do more,
he's above me now, ingesting, tensing.
I've let my life drift to a place with no
horizon, without vertical wonder.

The Hummingbird

This, in middle age. When all I've seen
has taken on a tired resemblance—
birds in their morning scattering. And men
in theirs. Songs for sleeping through. The chance
meeting, a splash of color that might open
the heart? Well, it's self-inflicted violence
to hope too long. And no shame to settle in
to what's at hand—an empty bed, and sense.

Then, this. This morning. The zinnias blurred
to desert sunset. And above them, almost still
in sharp relief: the ink-drop eye, the throat
rouged blue. I'd never seen a hummingbird—
not this close. I could've brushed its needle bill
with my fingertips, or palmed its buzzing heat.

Unemployments

My job is to tell you precisely where it hurts, which flexions
elicit pain, and your job is to tell me I can go run without
further damaging myself. You may not agree that this is your job.
And my job is to show up in boots and denim, and tan leather

and plaid, and y-fronts and tube socks. And your job will be
identical to my job. And your job will be to judge my job
well done, and my job will be to perform a winning indifference.
My job will be slow sip on a longneck. Will be beard and body

hair and brushed teeth. And yours, low lights, armpits, closed
eyes and tank top, will be hands behind your head. Or mine
will be couch and iPad-forefinger picture flicks. And offering
hurts, each a small vessel of identification careful not to brim over.

Or your job will be grimace, dying heart tissue, and shouting
discretely from the bathroom for help. Or rejecting food a little
sharply the second time. And my job will be eating food I
don't like. And my job will be dispensing half scoop of kibble,

while your job is insinuation between my ankles and sitting up
nearby, blinking softly. My job is stepping softly. Your job is

seismometer for my job. And my job is huffing. (I am
an expert huffer.) And your job is to appall with wry humor

and pictures of the porous bulbous-nosed politicians who vote
their interests. Your job is *whitemenwhitemenwhitemen,* while
mine is to forget that I am one. Mostly. Or my job is to smell it—
a scent registering dumbly in the mouth—that it's time to go,

and sit up slowly. And yours is lift yourself and easy shrug and
find my other sock. Your job is to foreclose the foreclosure
of possibility, transcendent or porcine, which happens also to be
my job. Soon my job will be to remember you, and your job will be

soil intensive. Your job, generosity in a general slackening.
Your job, a year-round forty degrees. And my job will be should-
have-said to the snappish air. Or your job is to wait for me to call,
and my job is to wait for you, which will present a problem.

Or yours is diagnosis; mine, manifestation. Or to enact—noun,
verb, and adjective—*cat.* And my job to admire your job. Cat, cat.
And the low chanting *Yit'gadal v'yit'kadash* at a hole in the ground.
And the yes, yes, no, yes, I'd very much not like to see you again.

To the Gentleman Who Asked for $500 to Cap My Chimney

Rain was getting in. A lot of it.
And there was evidence of bats.
And when I asked why it was
so damn expensive, you cited
careful measuring, a high-
quality cap, an exacting process.
Well, I did it myself.
I borrowed a thirty-foot ladder,
which was, at full extension,
barely tall enough. I clipped
the cap to my belt, glanced up—
a makeshift prayer—and step-
by-step ascended, looking only
at brick a few feet from my face.
I think often about vertical distances.
I think how quickly, if they were
horizontal, one might run them—
the six or seven miles up
that a plane might cruise,
how an able-bodied man
could swing it in three-quarters

of an hour. The half-mile
of a skyscraper, even
a middle-aged guy like me
could dash in three minutes
if he had to. And shorter—
four or five stories, enough
to kill you, certainly break
bone, you could run
in a minute, at most.
So my thirty feet: the length
of sidewalk in front of a house.
But how slow each step
as the ladder bowed inward
at the middle, where its halves
barely overlapped. I climbed
until there was no house, just
chimney. Then I climbed higher,
seeing the top and overtop, as if
I were the sun having finally risen.
Listen: the roof slipped away
at angles hitherto theoretical,
and as I screwed on the cap,
I dared to shift my eyes—
and glimpsed my neighbor
and his son, not quite insects
but, yes, small, pulling the edge

of a blue tarp mounded with leaves.
And, braver, I looked back
to see another neighbor, one
who lives behind me, who I've
never actually met, standing
in his yard, looking up
at me, and for a moment
our eyes met or could have
but didn't because he looked away.
But I saw him there in his
brown flannel, looking at my roof,
maybe wondering if I'd fall
or how I could be crazy enough
to do that without someone
down there bracing me.
And in that moment, I saw also
myself—from the ground,
just as he saw me—myself,
tiny, way up high, a man fussing
inscrutably on his chimney,
some little guy poised above
the neighborhood, the kind of guy
who does things like that—
practical, taciturn, who shrugs
when handed an impossibility
with directions in seven-point type

then gets to work. That's right,
the guy I am not, not remotely
in my belly aching and fears.
Have I mentioned that my hands
were, at this point, bloody
from scraping brick? I wiped them
on my shirt and realized
my neighbor would see that, too.
And as I finished screwing,
I knew—because people talk—
that all my neighbors would soon
understand that I was the one
who had done this work.
So I descended the ladder feeling
very much like the man I have
for a long time wanted to
go to bed with. And be. And you,
you with your blood-boiling
estimate, you inspired all that.
For that, certainly, you've earned
your five hundred bucks.

Praxis

Every pull up, every barbell, each inch
hoisted: the gripping fist, elbow planted
against the vinyl slant, atop the bench—
"preachers," we say, as if a prayer granted
this time, in real time: to move; to squat,
bar on your shoulders; to crunch, medicine
ball dense against the palms, then shot out
as your torso bursts from the decline.
It's not vanity, no drive for sex or power—
well, not just that—but sheer enacted will,
a beef with time, with gravity; each hour,
each ounce to know our push back; our kill-
or-be-killed heft shouldering against
its cackle and take, with every muscle tensed.

A Thought

Like a feather descending
in its back-and-forth motion,
slow twirl down to one
end of a balance, and that end
begins to sink—
but so slowly days pass,
an unscrolling of weather,
the view out the same window
over a series of months:
trees burst in lime-green flowers
so tiny that three or four buds
could rest on the tip of your thumb,
and then come rainy days,
darker leaves, and brightness
expanding like the yawning
of one just woken—
everything unfolding, changing.
And now you find it is
autumn, and somewhere
inside is a difference. A quiet,
monumental thing, difference.
Some dream that had long

seemed foundation wall
to a structure you'd hoped to build—
a Jeffersonian grandness.
You'd imagined marble, imagined
columns. But now it is you
who seem to find the structure
more trouble than it's worth, you
who might just, you decide, be
okay without so much grandiosity.
You even surprise yourself
with that word, *grandiosity*,
with its undertone of mocking.
What was it? A word, a look
from a man that wasn't—
you realized a moment too late—
directed at you. A casual
lapse that added its name
like another entry on a long
petition. No one, not even you
heard the creaking sweep,
the rusted iron gate
of your will. Though afterward,
at the window, you may
have wondered what bird
dropped that feather—

though so long ago now
there's no telling what kind,
or on its way to what country.

I Marry

I marry a column of air.
I marry my own
freedom, and at the altar
it and I merely brush
knuckles. I marry time
and march to the dais,
one forward step
as each second
ticks. I marry sex
and refuse to care who
steps into its body
as man after man
does. I marry a cat
or an impulse
like one, reclining
alone in darkness,
waking to its warm
breathing. I marry hot
liquid in winter,
curving around

the mug of it, and
in summer, the cold
grip of a plastic bottle
tipped over my lips.
I marry the silk
pucker of a coffin
lining, then file
for divorce and give
myself wholly to
well-fitting cotton
underwear and socks,
and am, for once,
convincingly held.
This man gets down
on one knee and raises
a small velvet box
into a wind that lifts it
from his fingers,
funneling it up
to the leaden sky.

Acknowledgments

My thanks to the journals in which these poems first appeared, sometimes in earlier versions:

Art & Understanding: "Days of 1993, '94, and '95"
Beloit Poetry Journal: "A Thought"
Birmingham Poetry Review: "Pinnacle"
Boulevard: "*In Medias Res*" and "Whose Eyes Dart Contagious Fire"
The Common: "Catherine the Great"
Crazyhorse: "The Hummingbird"
Epoch: "The Next World"
Green Mountains Review: "I Marry"
Hotel Amerika: "The Club, Houston," "I Go There," and "Afterward"
Jubilat: "Unemployments"
Kenyon Review: "In My Forty-Seventh Year" and "Catawba"
The Literary Review: "The Finish Carpenter"
The Massachusetts Review: "Thanksgiving at Mom's, That"
Measure: "Grandmother at the Stove"
The Minnesota Review: "The Magic of Macy's"
New England Review: "My Daughter Would"
Nimrod: "Math's Punishment"
Ninth Letter: "Facing It"
Notre Dame Review: "An Apology"
Pleiades: "Rosacea"
Ploughshares: "Heaven"
The Southampton Review: "Perhaps Because I Am Youngest"
The Southern Review: "My Mother's Novel"
The Sun: "To the Gentleman Who Asked for $500 to Cap My Chimney"
The Yale Review: "The Dogs of Sochi" and "Praxis"

"A Thought," "The Next World," and "*In Medias Res*" were reprinted by *Poetry Daily*.

"The Finish Carpenter" was reprinted by *Verse Daily*.

"The Magic of Macy's" was reprinted by *The Sun*.

Thanks also to the Connecticut Office of the Arts and Dean Katherine Black of the University of Hartford College of Arts and Sciences for grants that allowed me time to complete these poems, and to Richard Mathews, Joshua Steward, and the University of Tampa Press for such elegant design.

And finally, my gratitude to those who gave friendship and support: Bruce Cohen, Jim Finnegan and all the members of Brickwalk, Steve Green, Cate Marvin, Leslie McGrath, Kevin Prufer, Clare Rossini, Paul Simmons, Bryan Sinche, Sarah P. Strong, Amanda Walling, and Steven R. Young.

About the Author

Originally from Far Rockaway, New York, Benjamin S. Grossberg was educated at Rutgers and the University of Houston. From 2000 to 2008, he worked at Antioch College in Ohio, where he purchased a small farm and planted the Granny Smith orchard for which his second book, *Sweet Core Orchard*, was named. He is currently Director of Creative Writing and a Professor of English at the University of Hartford, in Hartford, Connecticut.

In addition to *Sweet Core Orchard* (University of Tampa Press, 2009), winner of the Tampa Review Prize for Poetry and a Lambda Literary Award, Ben is the author of *Space Traveler* (University of Tampa Press, 2014) and *Underwater Lengths in a Single Breath* (Ashland Poetry Press, 2007), winner of the Snyder Prize. He has also published two chapbooks, *An Elegy* (Jacar Press, 2016) and *The Auctioneer Bangs his Gavel* (Kent State University Press, 2006), and co-edited an anthology, *The Poetry of Capital* (University of Wisconsin Press, 2020). His poems have appeared widely, including in the Pushcart Prize and Best American Poetry anthologies, *Poetry Daily* and *Verse Daily*, and the magazines *The Paris Review, The Yale Review, Boulevard, Kenyon Review, New England Review, The Southern Review,* and *The Sun*.

Ben is also a distance runner and a vegetarian, and lives with a small black cat.

About the Book

My Husband Would is set in Garamond Premier Pro digital fonts, based on original metal types by Claude Garamond and Robert Granjon that were designed and cast in Paris, France, in the sixteenth century. The book was designed and typeset by Richard Mathews at the University of Tampa Press.

CPSIA information can be obtained
at www.ICGtesting.com
Printed in the USA
LVHW032108260223
740458LV00003B/699

9 781597 321822